THE
DEED

**Other Poetry Books by Carole Simmons Oles**

*The Loneliness Factor*
*Quarry*
*Night Watches: Inventions on the Life of Maria Mitchell*

# THE

# DEED

*poems by*

CAROLE SIMMONS OLES

*Carole Simmons Oles*

For Alice, with delight
in your work, your
presence.

Best wishes,
Carole
Cody's
Oct. 2, 1994

1991

LOUISIANA
STATE
UNIVERSITY
PRESS

BATON ROUGE
AND
LONDON

Copyright © 1981, 1983, 1984, 1985, 1986, 1987, 1988,1989, 1990, 1991
   by Carole Simmons Oles
Manufactured in the United States of America
First printing
00 99 98 97 96 95 94 93 92 91   5 4 3 2 1

Designer: *G. Phoebe*
Typeface: *Baskerville*
Typesetter: *G & S Typesetters, Inc.*
Printer and binder: *Thomson-Shore, Inc.*

Library of Congress Cataloging-in-Publication Data

Oles, Carole.
   The deed : poems / by Carole Simmons Oles.
      p.   cm.
   ISBN 0-8071-1701-3 (cloth). — ISBN 0-8071-1702-1 (paper)
   I. Title.
PS3565.L43D44   1991
811'.54—dc20                                    91-3931
                                                CIP

The poems noted first appeared in the following periodicals, sometimes in slightly different form: *Colorado Review*, "Letter to a High-School Friend, a Reformed Radical"; *Columbia Magazine*, "City of the Holy Flesh"; *Cream City Review*, "Visiting My Formerly Runaway Daughter and Her Husband at the Orchard in Vermont"; *Denver Quarterly*, "Quintet in C Major for Two Listeners"; *Georgia Review*, "Early"; *Indiana Review*, "On the Cliff Walk at Newport, Rhode Island, Thinking of Percy Bysshe Shelley"; *Kenyon Review*, Parts 3 and 5 of "Fugit Amor: A Sequence"; *New England Review/Bread Loaf Quarterly*, "In This Photo, Taken"; *New Virginia Review*, "On High Ground, River Thoughts"; *Overtures*, "Longing: After the Chinese Poet Hsiung-Hung"; *Ploughshares*, "They Set Out in Fog," "Four Bones for Late March," "The Radioactive Ball," and "Between Talcy and Mer"; *Poetry*, "Preparing for Weather," "Stitches," "Day Ten After Heart Surgery, Signing a Check," "The Gambler," "For Evelyn," "On Greyhound, Boston to New York," "Fugit Amor: A Sequence" (Part 1), "The Interpretation of Baseball," "High Heels," and "How He Celebrated Daily Mass"; *Poetry Miscellany*, "We Part the Waves on Main Street"; *Poetry Northwest*, "Postpartum II"; *Poets On*, "Territory"; *Prairie Schooner*, "In My Office, I Think I See," "Basil," "The Premonition," "Storm, Winter, Walking the Beach After a Separation," "Role Model," "Small Poem of Thanks," and "Sleeping Daughter"; *Southern Review*, "In Time, with Holsteins"; *TriQuarterly*, "To a Daughter at Fourteen, Forsaking the Violin" and "For the Drunk"; and *Women's Review of Books*, "Triptych, 1910."

The author wishes to thank Sweet Briar College for the Margaret Banister Writer's Residency, during which some of these poems were written.

for
Brian and Julia

# CONTENTS

THE
DEED

# IN TIME, WITH HOLSTEINS

*Can you not be decent? Can you not reserve your ardors*
*for something less unlovely?*
—William Carlos Williams


Windows of the breath, through which worlds pass,
my nose uplifts to serve me cow dung:
blown waves, a Holy Ghost igniting
air. My nose believes in honesty—this
pile which says the opposite of "waste."
The cows eat hay, make milk, bestow
fertility on corn. I'd like to follow
their ecological example. It's late,
but I observe them in their stanchions.
Attached to tubes they blink, watch back, and chew.
We begin to recognize each other. Vegetarian,
or nearly, I've calved and given my milk too.
In India, rites of penance and purification
use *pancagavya,* five products of the cow.

The *pancagavya,* five products of the cow,
are milk, curd, butter, urine, dung.
Milk for the amber cat who visits, yowling
till I surrender, kneel to give the blue
bowl of milk such as Solomon promised his tribes.
Curd for the runny Camembert my best
friend eats while waiting to hear "breast
cancer" or "benign." Curd for yogurt the wives
fermented two thousand years ago
in Kazakhstan with Lactobacillus bulgaris.
Butter on pumpkin bread, on Sabbath challah,
on thumbs which brush the oven's flaming eye.
Surely my friend will fly with me to Venice.
*Surely the churning of milk bringeth forth butter.*

The churning milk, the butter; fourth and fifth,
cow urine and dung, a huge philanthropy.
One half of every meal she renders daily,
bacteria and minerals, deposits in the bank of earth.
Eight percent of total body weight:
that makes about a hundred pounds a day.
I smell it from my porch, my bed, my sleep, the high
hill where stones recite lost names and dates.
At an Irish abbey once my sister installed
her footprint for posterity. Lifesize,

dung comforts me which, ignorant, I reviled.
I take the sacred wheel in through my nose
while swallows dip to skim the light off fields,
to pick the grain from mounds of dung, and rise.

I pick the gray from mounds of sunrise,
the cow gestalts from raveled mist. All right.
They're either white-on-black, or black-on-white.
I want to blink, friend, change your news.
Remember how it felt to breastfeed?—
such hard-rock swelling, the surge that made us drip.
At 4, the cows are hosed, then vacuum cups
like demi-octopi attack their teats.
Milking cows was always women's work.
Recently, a herd increased production more
than ten percent when women milked. "Speak
to cows as you would to ladies," said a farmer.
Today a calf has called me *Ma,* and licked
my teatish fingers wiggling through the boards.

My teatish fingers wiggling through the boards
cannot entice this newborn near. Stalled.
On her first two pairs of heels. The wall
for balance. Venturing out on the hard floor
as waves of tremors advance along her flank
    *oh, how to get off these stilts*
    *how did I get here . . . if I could waltz*
    *around, around—no I can't think*
    *what's next, so tired I am, so . . .*
oops and she folds at the first forward joint,
her rear follows, she's down. Bedded on straw.
There must be pillows somewhere. Yes, this loin
of matted hair. Her eyelids droop and sigh.
I smell digestion, milk, the lonely born.

They smell, digest. If men gave milk, bore
young, would they get gentler with their kind?
Or must they hurl their creatures to the ground
and burn their names in flesh—bull, cow,
woman, child? The cavemen hunted cows
with spears and captured them in pits. Before
money, cattle measured wealth, so later
they stood on coins. And what would I pay
eight percent of my total body weight
for, what would I spend to live? *On your hooves.*

*Stand it, stand up, even wobbling.* Right.
I'd spend what it took. The Pilgrims didn't have
cows at first. Most babies couldn't wait.
In spring, their parents gave them to the leaves.

In every season, pairings give their lives
to wind. I watch two hawks skydive, maneuver
thermals, conserve their strength. Cows, you foster
mothers: tranquilize us, feed us nerve.
For hard terrain, let calcium increase
our heartbeat's force, dilate our arteries.
"Most nearly perfect food," Hippocrates
pronounced—from young, to elders lacking teeth.
On my bookshelf we stand smiling. No fuse
is burning down behind us, no shade
is cast. We're calcium, sunlight, and eyes.
We're earrings, freckles, follicles. But cancer hid.
Lactose is used to form placebos:
*Whoever drinks me nothing will invade.*

Did I say "nothing" and "whoever"? *Placebo Domine
in regione vivorum, I shall please
the Lord in the land of the living.* Days
desert the calendar like film transitions. Hay
is rolled in golden rugs at pasture's edge
where cows move, stately in their bones.
"Dignified," my son says: *worthy.* Signs
of permanence, sufficiency. A nudge
toward purification. Great walking wardrobes
of coats that stretch on racks. Not found in fashion
ads or boxes at the Met. Their tails frayed ropes.
Their choreography of fringy looks. Penned,
crushed cheek by jowl, rump to earlobe
in ultimate togetherness. If they were less refined

that temperate togetherness would be inclined
to riot, break the barricade, bellow
*Grain!* Instead, the great heads float, they row.
Are they intelligent, or what? Pacifists of mind?
They trust each other more, they know themselves.
In eighteenth-century America
if city people wanted milk all winter
they had to own a cow. Imagine them
corralled on Commonwealth, on Madison.
(The homeless live there now.) Tell him what

we eat and Anthelme Brillat-Savarin
would tell us what we are. Illiterate
in Hindu Devi. Refugees from kin.
We rent this galaxy in which we ruminate.

They're determined to have fun.
The boy's 14 today. He's chosen
this trip North to where they lived
a life before him. There's the attic
in the gray Victorian where pigeons
nested until the cooing wasn't cute.
Where the father put his fist—why?—
through the wall. The owners' fights
rose through forced-air heating vents.

               At water's edge
a sailboat levitates on mist, seagulls
neither leave nor cease their flight.
All this salt air stings an open past.
At the coffeehouse they tune in 12
French tourists, discover they can translate
*Shall we sit in front or back?*
*You'll take spiced wine?*

               No connective
gets them to the boy's fall in mud
beneath the lighthouse, the father's
accusation. Sealed inside the moving car
they say the thing which cannot be unsaid,
she flings the car door wide, forcing
him to stop, someone innocent is crying,
earth is flowing in runnels to the sea . . .

               Going home
they transport silence. Dark now,
and the rain has gotten dangerous,
too many traveling close and fast.
She thinks of Jeffers at his ocean
". . . better for men To be few and live far
apart, where none could infect another . . ."
Beside the highway, lights from houses,
reference points along the night.

She knows today won't end: her father, dead,
comes reeling home every Christmas Eve.
How inscrutable, pronouns in her mother tongue.
She wants to say they love. To say how love,
like all their dreaming, mixes fog and salt.

Each time I send you into the sky
where money is made
I let you die.
It has little to do with the weather.

I settle the will, stare
into your closet, dispose of suits,
push some matters away until later.
An instant father, I can
advise the children without argument.
I have all the answers,

plus your half
of the queen-size bed, and
the nocturnal silence I elbowed you for
now an acreage too vast
to survey or build on.

Now you are a statue in the public garden
forever posed as *husband*
the way accident cast you.
You are among the perfect dead.
On my lunch hour I sit on the bench,
almost touching your bronze fingers
like Michelangelo near God.

I am just out of black,
beginning to sing in the shower,
when the door opens and someone like you is home
—poised for ribbons and balloons,
asking what happened
while he was gone.

*for my son*

Non-husband
   you can never divorce me.
      We're lifers since your birth,
         one act threw away the key.

This time you do the bleeding,
   allow me the forbidden:
      your hand.
        *Squeeze hard,* I say

while the Emergency Room doctor
   forces novocaine into your scalp.
      You clamp your jaw so tight
         I brace to hear the bone break.

He makes sutures fly
   acrobatic loops above your head
      before they seal the flaps.
         Toplit, he's supernatural

as Dr. Gross in Eakins' painting.
   You know the one—
      his blood-soaked cutting hand,
         and forehead under Godlight

the patient prone
   exhibiting the problem.
      That woman in black I call his wife.
      She has to turn away.

Something inside me kicks as I watch
from four storeys up the lean boy
in the parking lot, crimson knapsack
strapped to his narrow shoulders,
shapely dark head lowered, intent
on his stride toward the gray
foreign car. But he's not you.

You are hypothetical across the Atlantic
behind what my generation
of McCarthy-torn true believers
called The Iron Curtain.
It's thinned, become gauzy enough
for light, the smell of cabbage cooking,
the talk of students to seep through.

Twenty-one years ago you slid
across time, the thickest
head of hair in the nursery,
the largest hands. For piano,
"Für Elise," *Rachmaninoff* . . . (your piece
played yesterday on Public Radio) . . .

Now you ride a train, sipping black tea
and testing your Russian in Bulgaria.
A young woman with brown eyes
and a broad forehead teaches you new words.
The farms pass by your window
slowly, a worker looks up from his orchard
to wave. I'm a capitalist investing in you

as our remnant tribe plans the holidays
without you, peopling with fantasy
the added room, adopting in-laws,
your parents reverting to their parents.
We've pushed the button on our nuclear family,
the fallout will be felt for generations.

Now the student opens his car door,
throws his pack onto the passenger seat.
It's rained and the lot is studded with skies
which he breaks, turning out into traffic.
There's a knock at my door. *Come in*
I say to the presence.
Someone else's son sits down.

## TO A DAUGHTER AT FOURTEEN, FORSAKING THE VIOLIN

All year, Mozart went under
the sea of rock punk reggae
that crashed into your room every
night and wouldn't recede however
I sandbagged our shore
and swore to keep the house dry.
Your first violin, that halfsize
rented model, slipped out of tune
as you played Bach by ear
Suzuki method with forty other virtuosos
who couldn't tie their shoes.
Then such progress: your own
fiddle, the trellised notes you read,
recitals where I sat on hard chairs.
Your playing made me the kid.
*If I had those fingers!* . . .
Five of yours grasped my pinky,
the world before you grew teeth.
Okay. They're your fingers.
To paint the nails of, put rings on,
hold cigarettes in, make obscene
gestures or farewells with.

She in her dayglo orange crewcut
I, dun in all critical cover
save reflected glory that her hues emit.
Are we the same tribe, I and this womanling

the Pfc. wearing what used to be
designer pants, one incarnation ago dyed flu green
later reborn handpainted between wide stripes
a permanent marking of runes hieroglyphics
slogans that march over the difficult terrain
of her nevermore Mama's little baby's bum

which in the steamroom of July
beside a window overlooking towers of learning
the o.b. summoned (his partner's weekend on the Cape)
and while a radiance of neurons yelled URGENT
along my inner thighs, unready, resisting she
answered, finally, the hormones of convenience
and was born.

She the brother pronounced *dolly* wouldn't
lie still, go away, be merely pretty she who
now when the Pontiac slows down
and the all-American sticks his head out
confirming her opinions of the white man
to hoot *Ay freak, I like yuh haihcut*
and the spear sticks in my rib yet she endures
dear brave, most lonely dancer at full moon.

            I drum her home.

I didn't want to live with anything living.
I wanted three hospital rooms and a kitchen.
No traces, just cure.

No houseplants, I swore
but the ferns lined up outside Kroger's
like orphans yelling *me, me!*
Then there I was worrying about light,
walking my plant to follow the sun.
The next week I was feeding it.

Today I sunbathed on a hill
where planes flew low overhead
and bees clung to the flowers.
I put my shirt and pants to bed on the grass
and stretched on top of them as if
another me were laid out on my body—
or rising, leaving it for another dimension.

Children, one time in summer
I opened the screendoor
and heard a whir pass at my ear, hover
on the air before me as the hummingbird
reversed gear, flew back out
before I had let go the door.
That fast.

## VISITING MY FORMERLY RUNAWAY
## DAUGHTER AND HER HUSBAND
## AT THE ORCHARD IN VERMONT

*Let's drink to the hard-working people;*
*Let's drink to the salt of the earth.*
—The Rolling Stones

I need to explain to myself, so I tell my friends
you've dropped out of the middle class after one
short generation—mine, which rose on the spines
of working-class parents. Out of their neighborhoods,
their tax brackets, their broken English.

When I arrive up the dirt road, having stopped
for more detailed directions at the orchard
packinghouse, and having made nonetheless
one wrong turn, one stop at the wrong white
house, you are waiting. For me, and for
him, your husband two hours overdue, gone fishing.
*Oh daughter of the strong arm and sunburned nose.*
*Oh child of my disorderly bosom.*
I am glad to sit at your sticky table,
glad to drink the strong coffee you've brewed,
you remember *my* addiction.

We hear an engine panting uphill and then he
and his fishing mate, Larry from Florida,
reel into the kitchen, bravely displaying one
8-inch fish of unknown origin. Larry is happy,
and your man heavy-lidded—maybe there has been beer—
and when Larry smiles and speaks, his top teeth wag.
I can't understand more than one word in his ten
but his smile says fine, and I shake his hand
as calloused as my stone-carving, window-cleaning,
metal-lathing father's. Your Bobby gets Larry
to clean the fish, to show him how, and when
the dirty job is done—we three have turned
squeamish from the lesson—Bobby wraps
the fish in the daily newspaper
and throws it into the freezer, where intaglio
stories of x's drunk-driving charge, y's
9-pound boy, will solidify on its flank.
More coffee, Larry's departure, and a plan:
a tour of the orchard, the hidden sauna, the stream
then blueberry picking. But first

a snack of blueberries you two
have already gathered, set like sapphires
in vanilla yogurt unintentionally frozen. Delicious,
*delicious, and you, child, by my side.*

We stalk the rows of blueberry bushes, finding
what remains this late. The knock each globe
makes against cardboard reminds me of Sal's pail
in her story we read, heads touching over the page.
So many berries left, I am amazed
as we three spread out, calling to each other
from our separate camouflaging rows of green.
So many, and some so fat I can't believe
birds overlooked them, can't resist eating
them under the sun, under the pure blue of our reunion.
We combine our pickings—one luscious load—
and drive back to the bunkhouse.

*The two Bartlett pears on your windowsill*
*lean onto each other's shoulders like lovers.*
*They are almost ready, one is blushing, the light*
*forms an aura around them. One stands straighter,*
*seems to hold the other up more, but may*
*need the other's leaning to have it seem so.*

With dinner at the Jade Wah, we cannot
drink water because the supply is ruined
by industry. We wonder about the ice
in our soft drinks. I tell you of dark figures
squatting in ditches along the road from the airport
into the city of Calcutta; of your father fainting
on the bathroom tiles . . . *Your father—*
we blink once and pass him.
Last time we ate here, two summers ago, you
were living in a shack with six other people
and came to dinner barefoot. The management never flinched.

We reject our fortunes, rush down the highway
to the cinema to see *Parenthood.* You sit between us
holding hands with Bobby and me, as onscreen
families sandpaper each other. One daughter
wears your name, and elopes. Her parents are
divorced; the father, a dentist, loves his hand on the drill.
Neither of us is conned by the ending: a baby
for each happy pair. Retrograde, we agree.

Back in the bunkhouse, your boss and two other pickers
sit at the kitchen table and kibitz.
Paul has just returned from 3 months on a fishing boat
off the Aleutians and Terri, who smiles like a horizon,
follows crops across the continent.
Your boss says I look like your older sister.
I squirm when he jokes about elopement, cigarette breaks.
Soon it's bedtime—early. Work starts in the coolest
morning hours. You've made me a place upstairs:
a mattress on a boxspring on the floor. Across the hall,
you and Bobby will watch from your bed
sunrise over Monadnock. From my corner I see the shapes
of apple trees beyond the glass, silvered. I sleep.

By 5:30 the pans are rattling. Bobby cooks
blueberry pancakes so full of berries they clump
in the pan. He complains. I enjoy them. Good, strong
coffee and if I didn't have to leave, I'd stay,
try to pick apples. I don't want this to end now,
as I hug my girl and her husband.
I don't want them all to pile into the free,
battered Ford Fiesta, to follow them down
the rutted hill, out to the stop sign
she drives toward too fast,
to the packinghouse where they turn left
to get their orders for the day,
where she waves her hand out the window, her hand
toward which I, continuing straight, wave mine.

We walk twice around the same block.
A slack pace: June, and my mother's condition.
Such walls of roses! we stop to sniff.
No one is out in Brighton but flowers,
hanging pots of fuchsia, impatiens.
I am glad to walk so slowly.
Maybe if we smell each rose, then pause
to count each bay window, awning, porch swing,
we will never arrive at the hour.

Meanwhile, my back hurts.
I am carrying this, he has made me
his accomplice in the word
a person should not hear alone.
*Ask your daughter to come,* his nurse said.
Mother has studied the language of doctors
so she calls this visit routine.

I think of my first trip to France,
how I called my suitcase deaf instead of heavy.
I wish I were deaf, wish we were
in France where my mother has never
walked the City of Light, soared
with the buttresses of Notre Dame.
And I have left her God:
the saints and martyrs, smoky incense,
the disc glued to my tongue.

The word I think the doctor must say
grows between us, stinging nettles
she does not seem to see. If only I can
poison them, rip them out before.

Now we are stopped in a driveway
looking down to the garden protected
by a sheet-covered scarecrow whose arms
spread above the tomatoes,
and a white plaster Mary, her hands raised
to bless—what? That profusion? that growth?

## DAY TEN AFTER HEART SURGERY, SIGNING A CHECK

Bending forward on ratchets
as if she might again break
open breastbone to navel
or spring the ribcage
they had to saw through
to make good the heart inside

my mother signs on the correct line
an alien name—
like hers, but with consonants doubled
m's and n's drunk on their rises
like a needle stuck
loving one note

and I don't want to hear it
but I'm afraid of picking the arm up,
scratching the record.
I point, fetch her other glasses
and still the letters convene
too fast for her to grasp.

Seventy years ago
in the one-room schoolhouse
she learned words,
carried her name over snowdrifts,
gave it shining back
to her mother and father, earth-turners.

Now she must sign again
I say, banks are skeptics.
My breath climbs each extra curve
while we try to stay calm.
For this teaching, nothing
prepares me, nor for her
*I'm so stupid*

until here surfaces Miss Covell
who drilled me in penmanship.
*Slow,* I say. *Go slow, and count each hill*

as alive, beside me, needing cash
my mother signs her name.

**1   How the River Came into Our House**
On the dog's coat when he shook it
across the kitchen floor
as if it were horseflies;
in the chevrons of Canada geese
honking its name for their compass;
in the teenagers' throats
raucous with beer and hormones
as they fished off the bridge;
in the icy eyes of those
who had sailed it, helped by
a wind they supposed never would shift.

**2   A Mystery of the River**
One morning as usual, you
went to fetch the *Globe*
our paperboy tossed to that far border of lawn
and bending there
you saw the fish staring back
shocked, as if it had been released
from a high branch of the oak.
The river was telling
us then about things
where they didn't belong.

**3   How I Went into the River**
We had just pushed off from the dock
and the canoe seemed to be turning its ankle.
I let it, I didn't struggle. I was the leg
attached, rotating. Wet.
My knapsack floated within reach
and our sandwiches stayed dry.
Who had seen? I could laugh, and shiver.
Nearby, a child asked, "Why
did she do that?"

The second time, I meant to put myself in.
It was evening, we had finished the wine.
Late August pasted itself on our flesh.
The river was unclean, but no harm:
for a second, clothed, I slid down.
My white T-shirt turned tan,
brown flora tattooed my arms.
I rose from the foul bath grinning, refreshed.

### 4   How Else the River Came into Our House, and Another Mystery of the River

No door I closed or didn't
could keep that river out.

A man sits close to the river.
Gone from him his beloved
who praised water which lifted her
from herself, bore the leaden
limbs that could not climb.
"The Beast," she called the M.S.
giving it a shape to fight.
But that other was like polluted air.
No escaping, except not breathe.

Thus abandoned by God, in sickness, in sickness . . .
and the river let her in.
I am telling this because the river keeps every secret,
or has no memory.

The man has all memory.
All wounds the river suffers not
open in him.
It should have refused, dried up, frozen solid again
that first day of spring
when it saw her resolute step
her eyes focused on a point on the gray horizon
where the beginning of sky fused
with the end of land and the river
which was letting her in.
Which was not a boat
not a lover or child
nor child's child—
none of these was cold enough
none could carry a woman far enough
from her first and last sorrows.

Someone said "took her life"
as if she had stolen.
Someone answered, *It was hers.*

You'd lift the smell onto your fingers,
wear it for hours like exotic perfume.
Ground with mortar and pestle, mixed
with olive oil, grated cheese, pignoli
at the end of summer, your frozen balm
in recycled jars lined up like national
reserves to be called in January.

You and I didn't believe in saints. We believed in food.
We sat next to your wood-burning stove
while the soup kettle boiled. We weren't on our knees.

Some visceral brain, some central intelligence of loss
fed me pesto tonight,
this first anniversary of your death.
I want to call you, say *linden tree, grandchild,*
*Vassar College* where I imagined you
in that library like a church,
light falling across your brown curls,
your smile as you read
the Wife of Bath's Prologue.

Friend, some days you are pungent. Just
under melting winter, you crown through
the first immoderate spring day.

        Basil leaves, olive oil, grated cheese, pignoli:
I take them onto my tongue this season
of my Easter, your Passover. Shelley, come.
Sit in your chair.

# THE PREMONITION

I am wheeling my grocery cart
into the sunshine, parking it
beside the trunk of my car to unload
when the crone with clipped
white bristles on her chin,
dirty white strands pasted to her skull
springs up before me,
hunger in her outstretched palm.
                                    I taste
pennies as the celery luxuriantly blooms,
the animal flesh strains
under its plastic tourniquet.

I plunge into the night of my wallet
to get the smallest bill then look,
make myself look, at her—the white patchy
nose and cheeks: as if frostbite struck
in the mild southern fall,
the cut over one eye, the stubble
that could scour a pot,
the teeth a message in Morse code.

What's the point, I think
when the machinery of state grinds on,
she not so much as a shoe to sabotage it.
Will my money pour her booze? Who wouldn't
crawl into that warm dark tunnel.

Woman, am I finished with you now
as I lift bag after bag into the trunk
taking care so nothing will spill, or break.

### The Marriage Bone
Once broken it tends to give
under pressure. Though the knit serves
the gait will always be slightly
protective, the limb will remember
a fault line, the snap of its failing.
It may bear your weight cunningly
down the avenues of custom
so that no one else notices.
Left/right, left/right—walk you will
but not sport freely. Perhaps not dance.

### The Truth Bone
Mine you say
—No, mine
and he grabs it,
chews until it's all gone.
In the dim light
you may think you've imagined
that hard white teether.
He digs another from his pocket
and spends it on you
like small change for a hustler.
It splinters in your hands.

### The Who Cares Bone
You know you left it right here
but the table is empty
the cupboard is bare.
Panic begins in your chest
and pushes up toward your hairline
as you check under the sink,
behind the framed photos,
inside the medicine cabinet.
Where the hell did you put it?
Aahh, who cares.
You reach out the window
for that one bird's armature of song.

### The What Next Bone
It's invisible now.
You have to construct it from droppings
on the brick path, those red nibs
rained down like the trees' bloodletting.
You have to extrapolate it from

the downy woodpecker's red throat and crown
startling as accident along the bare branches.
You have to stand on the set bone
and walk, starting here. Wherever
you go will be somewhere.
You'll kick something with your foot
after it almost trips you:
the bone of what's next.
You'll begin to find its relatives.
You'll assemble them in the shape of a life.

Fallen leaves big as a man's face
look up from the path.

You and I were a house, then
a room, finally a sill.
Caterpillars left their husks
on our back.

But sometimes when we looked away
or listened to light
stir the oak
the ancient song called us.
Then we rose and swayed,
tall grasses carrying a single current.

Until again that prince rode
in from the provinces
pushed open the door, threw
its shadow across the table
where we broke
and broke bread.

# THE GAMBLER

*En route via Reno, Nevada*

Last onto the plane, now he slides
to a stop in the aisle beside me,
a batter reaching home.
The fat woman in his window seat
will have to move. Then he
can slip past me like water over rock.
He is the color of the Mississippi
and dressed all in caramel sugar.

There's a neutral zone between us
but something keeps sneaking across.
His big white hot neon smile.
*I saw you in the bar,*
he unbuttons the news.
No one knows me on this plane.
His smile circles—a barracuda perhaps
but gee I like this fish.

*Come with me to Reno for two days,*
he doesn't even whisper.
*Bring me luck at the table*
and he lists what we'll do
leaving out oh well, that.

I play it cool, smile my own circles.
I'll think about it, and meanwhile he hopes
someone fine is waiting for me—
a little harpoon into my flank.
Of course I wouldn't
but I am thinking the kind
of woman who would.

His voice pours me amber whiskey.
His diamonds and gold flash
in the overhead reading light.
He rests his hand on the velour seat
between us, spreading his fingers, stretching
to play a chord.

The wind wanted to hurl us back where we came from
but we pressed against it, threw all our weight
behind each step onto the wet sand while the whole
Atlantic repeated go back go back from the line
it staked
        but we needed to pivot wide from the hips with
each step, insisting against a common obstruction.
Which one of us would it trip? Who would tire, turn,
get into the car first?
        The beach was littered:
chunks of armor—molting season for horseshoe crabs
those tanks with whips and eyes, and mermaids' purses,
the wealth of generations squandered, tangled in seaweed.
Spume blew a path across ours
                like chemical warfare
and I mimicked a shellfish inside the hood of my parka,
cinching the cord till a nose, two lower eyelids barely
protruded and still the wind rammed in. Your hair flew
in tattered flags. Your ears, once shells with songs
in them, glowed now like something we'd eat.
        In one resort hotel, some sliding glass doors
had blown out and curtains escaped over the balcony,
climbed back again before they were missed.
The guests had left in a hurry after clenched teeth,
a hand pinning a wrist to the jamb. Steel
girders angled out from one rooftop like knives in the bull.
Pulleys and scaffolding slammed against concrete.
                I was thinking let's
go as far as the jetty, but you said it, believing it farther
than I wanted to go, while I'd been thinking it not
far enough for you. So it seemed to each of us
a treaty. We signed it. Overhead the seagulls pushed
just as deliberately single file.
        Then, down the beach a surfer
sheathed in bright green raised his board like a shield
and strode to the water. The waves wouldn't stop frowning.
We both said crazy. No one should be out in this alone.

The glass frog of rainforests
glows like a halo,
embryonic as roe.
Nothing chameleon about him,
no masquerading wherever he clings.
Not to be worn as a figleaf
to hide any nakedness,
not trapped in stone near the pond.
He sees through himself:
green bones, and the single
red road to the City.

Hold him up,
let light stream across
93 million cold miles to project
upside-down in Lotus position—
    the new man
    so brave
    his heart is exposed.

before Hiroshima, radiation sickness, *hibakusha*
before the killing showers
before the pollution and reclamation of the Hudson
before the Imperial Woodpecker became extinct
before a man walked on the moon
before the assassinations, the resignation
before the Salk Vaccine, before AIDS
and Roe vs. Wade
before Watts and Black Panthers and Weathermen
before skinheads
before my mother's tonsillectomy, hysterectomy
exploratory stomach surgery, open-heart surgery
before removal of the melanoma on her cheek
(a beauty spot, then a too-emphatic period)
before she gave back a new son
before she cried at the porcelain table
before I panted, bore down, and delivered
before her grandchildren devoured her cookies
brought forth music with their own twenty fingers, drove vans
made etchings, spoke foreign languages
did drugs, won prizes, crossed continents—

in this photo my mother stands at 23
wearing a pullover and baggy trousers
gone in and out of fashion three times now
she stands among trees, all shades
of gray stippled leaves
with sunlight before her, her head tilted down
as she leans her cheek against the baby's
whom her arms ferociously enclose.

Never have I been so thoughtless,
so happy to be held.

We are being ourselves at your pond's edge,
me taking swimsuit cover
you nude, shaving your legs.

While the sun beats time
we wash our woes in the lap lap
launching husbands, sons, daughters
toward the other shore.
Like two veteran schoolmarms
we take attendance by counting the absent

and I am in that other July we rested
among the antiquities at Gardner Museum
where we'd gone having sprung you
from Beth Israel Hospital.
Where we sat on the wall and wept
for what the experts would do to your heart
to your heart in twenty-four hours.

But you—we—still miraculously present,
have another summer full on our backs.

Friend, in these our bodies' light ships
some picture we must make:
me bound in embarrassing shame
and you taking off even your hair.

When a woman walks in the woods
she will mark her territory by crouching.
In books I even like
men pee against trees, over the sides of boats,
pee to hose out their fires.
They mark words as *his.*

          I claim this paper for my tree.

Here women pee in the open,
within the compass of their crouch.
They do this in the attitude of birth—
before, that is, medicine men
told them to lie down
and cross gravity.

Not for height or distance,
not as shot-putters measure
the hurler's biceps, and not
sending a missile over the land.
But to wet a place deeply.
The issue foams between their planted feet.

From where they crouch they see
the eft ignite a rock,
the Amanita raise warning.
Trillium, the endangered,
wilts quickly if taken
for bouquets.

# FOR EVELYN

*Female dolls in their nakedness are the most female things*
*on earth.*
—Katherine Mansfield, *1921*

I named you for Evelyn Keyes
who played roles like the patient wife
of a San Quentin lifer,
the Mom of a freckle-faced boy.

But my Evelyn, you would not be blonde.
Your black hair was the fur
of cat or sheep or something wilder.
You would not have open blue eyes.
Amber, yours could close, look sideways.

You were so not me I had to love you.
Still I improved on your femininity
with "Windsor Rose" from my aunt's vanity
table, painted your wooden nails
and your minuscule

lips, which anyway stayed shut
before I glossed them tight.
No you weren't one of those criers
with the tin plate in their chests
that made them say Wanh or Ma-maanh.

Which brings me to your
body. Realism ended at the head and limbs.
Thigh to neck, mum
was the word. You were a stuffed cushion,
a female *thing* whose linen-
covered "body" was just more dress.

No wonder you looked surprised.
Where were your nipples, navel, nether lips?
your buttocks and armpits?
No wonder you looked into corners,
maybe that's where they hid.

Evelyn, we held each other in my bed.
Whoever took them might come back for more.

*New Orleans, Mardi Gras*

At every corner, cops patrol in pairs.
Our first night, sirens haul us
in and out of dreams. We improvise
the crimes—coke, theft, murder—
until day, when helicopters
lettered SHERIFF fan the sky.

On Royal Street a blond in shorts
is frisked to his athletic socks.
Three black men unfurl across
a doorway in the early heat.
Before we pass, they leave:
we must be dangerous.

At the Battle of New Orleans
General Jackson ordered his men
to cut the sugar cane
in spears to stop the British.

In Jackson Square now, no one's
stopped. Dixieland, bare breasts,
face-painting, mooning from a balcony,
Mozart on the glass harmonica,
spoon-playing by the dervish,

even God is here, in the steeple
of St. Louis Cathedral, watching
with his eye, the clock.
*Ego sum via et veritas et vita*
echoes in gold leaf above the altar.
A man pisses against the transept wall.

Girls crowned with floral wreaths
parade their innocence along the levee.
A Christian with a mike harangues
us all to call on Jesus. We turn
the other cheek, the Mississippi yawns . . .

*we're a paraplegic in his wheelchair,*
*whose jokeshop penis towers*
*from his lap, circled with the necklaces*
*of Mardi Gras, a game of ring-toss*

*and a beauty in shocking pink*
*coy at first, refusing, who yanks*
*her dress down to serve the crowd*
*the "Tits" it yells for,*
*St. John's head on a plate*

When Zulu went bare-breasted
white men said Sin.
Today the paper says
"Many New Orleans blacks are light-skinned
and must wear blackface in the Zulu floats."

*we're the lamé women of every sex*
*the drunk asleep on garbage*
*the drunk who wants a match*
*we're the voyeur at our window*

Meanwhile the Christian passes flyers.
"Your future foretold:
        'He who has Christ will live forever in heaven.
        He who has not Christ will spend eternity in hell.'"

This isn't hell or heaven
but the place they meet, a seam
that joins the two sides of a shirt.

*we put it on*

We're speeding through the bombed-out Bronx—
there go the boarded storefronts,
spray-painted walls that say
BECOME CATHOLIC
as if it were a way downtown.

My seatmate, touring from New Zealand,
wants to know
do any whites live in Harlem.

In the 60s I spent one weekend
here with the American Friends.
I did it for a boy.
We undergrad reformers walked the streets
with our guide, a black man
built like an el pillar.
We tried to be white flags
in the middle of war.

Now my seatmate's pointing to
a tenement six stories high
with concrete blocks in its windows.
Quick I make it into architecture:
how noble the pediment
above each former glass.
Isn't this why I went to college—

to see life beat art at symbols,
see art beat the hell out of life?

Blame Schubert. Liszt said he was
*le musicien le plus poète qui fût jamais.*
Implicate the double cello.
Add the arrangement of the chairs,
the walnut wainscot, vaulted roof,
the leaded glass where moonlight searched
and pinned them like a mortal threat.
This was no perfume ad.
The music surmounted all intelligence,
confessed them, opened
them and stitched itself inside.
Who wouldn't follow it off a cliff
and kiss the rocks?
Oh those sleeping dogs, the senses!
Go back to just before *cantabile*—
make the victims leave their seats
and part, churn gravel, not stop, and live.
Then burn down the gazebo.
Every stave.

## 1   Fugit Amor

*after Rodin,* The Gates of Hell

The lover's flight seems launched underwater—
she flutter kicks, glides out beneath
him. Where back to back they held together,

now, eyes closed, she holds her breath
and rides her elbows upwards even as he
tries to keep her there, fastening his left

hand to her right breast, stretching high
his right hand to collar her, to clutch
or pull her hair; but no bereft display

of pectorals, biceps pulls her home, his touch
the springboard she arcs from, toward air
where the *O, Amor* of his mouth can't reach.

Meanwhile certain thoughts, dreams, bore
through the top of her head, she needs both hands
to bury them, contain her mind before

this perversion explodes it. A critic finds
"this ill-mated pair represents
humanity without moral love," bound

forever to be disuniting, in bronze.
She's still lashed to and fleeing him at once.

## 2   Nothing Possessed

> *Nothing possessed rest, not even death; for decay,*
> *too, meant movement, dead matter still subject*
> *to life.*
> —Rainer Maria Rilke, *Rodin*

So even as she thinks *No autopsy,*
*just bury the body,* thought raises it.
Places it on this square then that; deploys

it around the board, demands that she forfeit
pieces. When her father died, in those
months just after, she felt him more present

than for decades, a still subject who rose
in her constructions, renovations. Now,
her marriage leveled, she finds no repose—

memory squares the corners, lie after lie.
The dotted line leads straight here. She'll sign.
If nature speaks, can she hear what it says?

Sprawled in winter woods, the dead tree shines
with beetles, fungi leaving footprints on decay.
Poured honey heats the swarming carbons,

the tree is repossessed by hills and gullies.
And by her retinas and neural paths,
her nose. Threading through her lacework bronchi,

flung out on each wing of her breath.
*To life,* all matter says. *Breathe.*

### 3   She Who Was Once the Helmet-Maker's Beautiful Wife

*after the bronze by Rodin*

*When I think, alas! of the good times,*
*what used to be, what it's become . . .*
—François Villon, *"The Regrets of the Helmet-Maker's*
*Beautiful Wife"*

Balloon in the act of collapsing, she's saved
by her knees, a ledge jutting from rock
she hurts to sit down on. No drapery hides

what's left of her lap. Where breasts once obstructed
her view, now they lie flat as cutlets,
a button on each, as her head bends toward crotch,

that good time. Where belly stretched and inflated,
spanned a world for the baby inside, the roof
has caved in. It hangs like a valance in pleats.

But she still has her bones: shelf
of sternum; shoulder blades and honed elbows;
backbone ridges like dangerous reefs.

Right arm behind, is she fending off blows?
Maybe her lower back aches. Her hand's
nailed to the cross of her past. What use

were his helmets? They saved not one son,
one beauty of yesteryear. Her,
she's a sunken galleon. Wait. She's not done.

See how force concentrates in that gesture.
Her splayed fingers call, and you hear.

## 4 In the Law Office

*Lasciate ogni speranza, voi ch'entrate.*
—Dante, *The Inferno*

She will be offered coffee with real cream
no "non-dairy product," she
will be offered the new *People* magazine

to help her pass these minutes of waiting, so-
awkward minutes during which indecision
may raise her from the chair, dance her to

the elevator where she'll press the arrow down,
whirl through glass revolving doors to the world
where hope still may fly but has more often

minced on pavement, perched high to defile
the granite of commerce, the bold heroes of state.
She thinks she's already done it, climbing uphill

—*Lasciate ogni speranza*—to Court Street.
Now at the round table, opposite counsel,
she's about to give the order, let this hardhat

throw the lever, pitch the wrecking ball
like medieval torture. She thought she'd felt
all its forms, but this is a new circle:

to speak in numbers and safe-deposit vaults.
Silk falls from her body. She is bone and regret
among these reflectors, these glaciers of salt.

## 5   The Caryatid Fallen Carrying Her Stone

> *The figure bears its burden as we bear the impossible in*
> *dreams from which we can find no escape.*
> —Rainer Maria Rilke, *Rodin*

The temple's reduced to one stone. All tension
resides in her right hand
holding it up, being weighed down.

The rest of her's already folded.
A leg angled out, she sits embracing
the other knee. That hug is a pillow

her head can press into, displacing
its weight, which adds to the stone's. A flutter:
the bird who nests behind her face . . .

*emerald wings and black head hover*
*while in the next room two "friends" entwine*
*and she can hear the bird drink nectar*

*at her throat; if her eyes fly open*
*it will peck them, as vultures strip*
*the newborn calf before the farmer lifts his gun . . .*

*she's driving children over the mountain draped*
*in snow and night, when half the steering wheel*
*breaks off and turns to cellophane—how can they sleep*

*where will they stay, how many more miles . . .*

Stones like this one may take years to fall.

## ON THE CLIFF WALK AT NEWPORT, RHODE
## ISLAND, THINKING OF PERCY BYSSHE SHELLEY

The house of stone turns its back on town
to govern an Atlantic even sky can't stop.
Big as a museum, it keeps us off the lawn
with chain-link fences camouflaged by rosehips.
Presiding from this height it says *Look on*
*my works, ye Mighty, and despair!* I do,
counting forty windows, six French doors,
a dozen chimneys. Gone, the men who
ushered progress here, those individuals;
who breakfasted on the green, debating wars
their women wouldn't understand. Farewell.
The waves still fling their ermine to the land,
refine the rocks colliding in their pull—
a loud applause that steadily makes sand.

## LETTER TO A HIGH-SCHOOL FRIEND,
## A REFORMED RADICAL

In senior year, your hair revolted too,
overthrew crewcut and ducktail.
Your hair wrote its private manifesto
most girls gladly would have signed.

There was no excess in your body,
each part accorded its ability.
You didn't need great height.
When you'd dispute, you seemed to smile.
Spittle oiled the corners of your mouth
and kept us listening.
You'd wave and pace,
outmaneuver your opponent.

Something was almost whispered
in the corridors of learning, something
about your parents, who wore Space Shoes
and rode to Lewisohn for concerts
while The Inquisitor accused.

In the Sunday magazine now you recant
your unenlightened old beliefs.
You have a pool in your backyard.
You wear a tie—I bet you "dine."
O.K., but I'm sad
how gray fur overgrows
your fiery cheeks, the family chin.

*with the women's college Outing Club*

## Prologue

We're all in karst. That's pitted land:
shafts and sinkholes, water,
long alleys with no way out. *Karst—*
the consonants of rheumy throat-clearing
or someone cursed. Like
Christ, or Kurtz.

## The Descent

We enter down the sinkhole with sides so steep
we have to ski, traverse the slope.
Like motes, we drift into the yawn
and stand in twilight.
Moving deeper, still seeing our way,
I turn. The sinkhole wall cross-sections earth,
roots ripped and jutting. Where the moon should
hang, tree branches throw a snare.
A few feet down, and then no sky.
A wedge of light on rock, like memory:
Grandpa's cellar and the slanted door,
slamming overhead.
I see water not stopping
at my neck, me flailing, no ark.

## Within

Leaning back against the angle of precipitation,
slow-motion we advance on grease.
Our bodies signal caution while the headlamps
roll round welcomes out before us.
We find a millipede, and spotlight every
segment's roseate pearl,
that steady progress on thirty pairs of legs.
Too close overhead hang sleeping bats.
We swerve our lights, our body heat away.
If waked too soon, they'll starve.
Then, headlamps off, we see
black velvet where our hands are raised.
Our words are blotted up. Only water speaks,
a measured leak. This is how time sounds.

Above us, once-rushing currents have carved
Art Deco swirls in limestone.
In utero, I must have seen
the red dome of my mother,
heard the hymn of blood through veins.
I gaze here like the first explorer
but farther on, fingers have touched the tarry walls,
stripped their dew, a firmament.
The oily messages can never be erased:
> *Fred and Sue. 1966. Eat shit.*

## Balance

Down further: wetter, muddier.
Where we have to ford the stream
the far shore rises, a beginner's slope in freezing rain.
We need the other's hand as much as ours,
we plant her as if she were ourself.
Soon, we reach a pass so slippery
we go down on hands and knees along a ridge,
crawling to the steady drum of water,
and castanets: our hats against jutting rock.
We move one segment at
a time, strain to multiply our grasp.
The circle of our concentration three dim
holds ahead, we learn
complete attendance in this moment. All feeling
means shins and knees and clutch
along this ragged ledge.
Nothing happened, nothing will.
It only matters not now to fall.

## Birth

Hoisting on women's arms like fins, scrambling
for a foothold, twisting torso for a slot
as toe-brace, balancing the other knee,
lower back jammed on mudslick walls, breath
too huge and ricocheting
                    I praise the knob to grope
and praise the floating hand that looms
before my lamp to drag me up
the last push of the bone canal.

So trust flattens the body against itself
to reach another dark.

In a niche, enshrined,
three Old Milwaukee empties.

## The Ruler
Now space, with vaulted roof where,
patterned by the waters, a full moon sails.
A broad stream saves
the tubes where bat sopranos trill.

In pleated robes and grand indifference,
presides a Pharaoh fifteen feet tall—
each inch counts off a hundred years.
One last squeeze upward from this king
we stand amid subtropic vegetation,
stalactites like banana leaves,
a pearly pendant at each tip.
Along the walls, more wet constellations.
Our hands are steaming brews,
calories swirl in haloed light. But
someone's dared to cross the chasm,
break two thousand years of limestone off
to make himself a sceptre.

## The Surface
On my mother's tempered body
purple roads where they've gone in
for trophies or attached synthetics.

A pinhole shines far up, the eye
we climb towards from this heart
of broken stones, stars of dew fallen prostrate,
obscurest shelves proclaiming man.

John Muir wrote *"It is a good thing
even to creep like worms into dark holes
and caverns underground, to see
better what the sun sees on our return
to common every-day beauty."*

Worming into sun glare,
squinting at each other's mud and sweat
we're wobbly, but we stand here where we can—
this one, precarious, female globe.

It took time to figure out who was missing
from the dream ballclub that paraded
through the dark in uniforms and numbers
holding up posters of the lost teammate
as if campaigning for their man.

I had to walk the dream railroad track again
where my son followed me at first, then took
the lead, balanced, leaped forward over the ties,
*poof*—gone!
And to sit with the inquisitor who wore
my dachshund around his neck like a precious
fur with lacquered eyes.

I had to listen then to memory,
your fastball, your grand slams out of the park.
And go back to the bleachers at Yankee Stadium
where you took me at 7 though I was not the son
whose heart, that sly courser, unseated him.
He was the one you saved your prize for,
the baseball Babe Ruth signed.
You tried to show me what you saw
but I was gabbing about something else:
another hotdog, how many more minutes.

It took time, Father, to see
you swinging, connecting.

I caught it
and screamed for water.

Someone carried a pail,
I plunged my hands in.
The water boiled.
I wore violet gloves beaded with glass.

Now what do I do with this water.
How can I pick the pail up,
where should I set it.
How to turn doorknobs and enter rooms
and not lift my child.

Is it too late to cut them off.
Where will I bury them.
If I burn them, who
will breathe the air of their burning.

Throw them into the ozone.
Ship them to Mars,

these death hands.

No pockets will have
them.

**SLEEPING DAUGHTER**

*The daughter of Edward J. Martin, a Marinette ex-*
*alderman, has awakened after sleeping nearly a week.*
*During that time her slumber was wholly unbroken and*
*the strongest efforts of her attendants failed to waken her.*
*Physicians ascribe her strange condition to a sort of*
*nervous prostration due in a measure to the death of her*
*mother last summer and a fright she received. . . . She is*
*17 years old.*
—*1899 state records, quoted in*
Michael Lesy, *Wisconsin Death Trip*

With a noose around his heart
poor father wandered room to room
searching for her: an innocent man
sentenced to life.
I had the little ones to distract
from her absence. Music had fled.
Now the birds' anthems struck our ears
like the schoolmaster's whip
as another day dared begin.

After the children had left for school
I stood at the soapstone sink
and watched them get smaller,
colored confetti blowing across the snow.
And all at once the whole length of him
was against me, pressing so hard my breath
would not come, the last of it
gone out on my cry. I thought I was dreaming,
the snowfield erupted in black puffs
as I struggled to make sense.
His hands leapt like flames over parts of me
no one had ever touched, not since
I began to bleed. This could not be.
I wanted to roll back this day
like a huge boulder into the mouth of a bear's cave,
wanted to undo these moments outside time.
*Help me,* he moaned as I turned to face him
who had made me along with the woman
newly gone from us all. *No!*
my mind shouted but when I opened my mouth
no sound came out—like the lamb last spring
hanged on the barbed wire which meant to secure it.
Now I saw his face, eyes rolled back, lips hanging

like the idiot boy from Merrill. I saw logs float
down the river, saw the men hammering
fenceposts, saw their 4-pound sledge open a log
I saw Mrs. Lundgren the midwife catching John
from the swollen almond that split
between Mother's thighs—all this I saw
in that instant when Papa clamped me
as for the worst thrashing. My knees unlocked
and the kitchen rose as I sank through the floorboards
down into the dirt cellar with stored grain,
rats, and in my nose held the stench of things
sodden and decayed, I fell further down
through the floor of that cellar
as earth resumed its shape over me
—I had never walked there—and the worm sang
and the beetle clicked, hidden in that deeper black
where I fell towards Mother.

And when I stopped at the core, packed into darkness
I felt the weight of a house on my chest, heard bones
splinter like teacups against a wall
I lay self-contained as a stone, mindless of day and night
until before me a silver thread shone, a snail's map
and I grasped it, pulled myself hand over slippery hand
to reach the lid of earth
where her voice prayed me *Laura! climb back.*

Opening my eyes,
I could not tell the distance of objects
nor whose bed, curtains, basin surrounded me.
Who were these men, pencils in hand, writing
as I blinked and moved my lips to speak
letting out a sound like a jail door opened slowly
against great resistance. I could not feel
where was my body.
Could as easily have lifted a barn ridgepole
as my arm which drew a white line
down the quilt, ended in a cluster of cornsilk.
Who was this man whose eyes pinned my face,
whose tangled beard hung past
the third button of his faded shirt?
I spat my rusty word, and woke again.

The first time I wore really high heels—
three inchers, I mean—was at Sunnyside Garden
the fall of my first Presidential
vote, the year John F. Kennedy ran.
Smooth magenta leather with a bow
pointing the instep. The same color
as one thread in my plaid bolero
and requiring certain adjustments of posture,
certain regressive tendencies. Oh but Jack was a man
women would suffer high heels for,
a man who would lift us from kitchens,
transport us to Ghana in the Peace Corps.
Politics had never been so romantic.
Never so handsomely had a man embodied our ideals.
There in Queens, our long wait was the kid
that shook the bottle of warm Coke
that was the crowd.
Finally the men in blue nodded, uncapped
us, and we sprayed through the doors.
I began to understand the texts: *mass movement,
mass hysteria* but I was young, we were all immortal.
He arrived late and when the sirens
sang him in he strode, waving, down the aisle,
climbed into the ring, touched the microphones,
and as he moved into the light
we thousands in shadow rose cheering. I stood on
my toes in my high heels to get a clearer view.
He looked so small! so far away, until
he spoke. My feet would hurt in those shoes
but not now. Now we were using the heels
of our stinging hands to applaud.
Jack was better than any church.
He didn't have to tell us we were bad
to make the good a country we could reach.
I soon came off my high heels. Married a not-tall
man. We were living by the ocean when the news hit.
We didn't know where to walk to get well,
didn't care what we wore on our feet.

Sometimes I feel *down at the heels*
or that the nation's full of *heels*.
Or I want to *lay by the heels* all villains, Shakespeare-style.

High heels haven't ever come back big. They wreck
the spine, the arches. They're not for women
who stand on their feet and walk
on the world's troublestones.

Here 40 years ago on moonless nights
pilots cut their engines
and Allies parachuted down.
I know from movies
the farmer's lantern, the password.

In July now, irrigation sprays
fan the fields with light,
tiny mirrors that rise, arc, shatter
the heat-stunned afternoon.

Along the unswerving road
someone has planted roses—for miles,
alternate sides the way a flowergirl
scatters petals for the bride and groom.
The French are like this with roads.
Everywhere ranks of poplars converge
on horizons: marching, but art.

Talcy is a village of 223 people
and a 13th-century château
where Ronsard courted Cassandra.
The German cyclist is headed there too.
We're all foreign, with time
to stop for this photo.

The two hourglass shapes you see
in the haze are the nuclear
power plant, France of the future.
That's us beside roses and cornfields,
beside ourselves listening
to nothing spread its wings.

*After hearing the priest on his months as hostage*

What then would I daily celebrate
in the dark night of my captivity, blind-
folded, chained to the radiator? What rite
could keep me whole in my mind?
Forbidden to sing, lest voice be a gate
I could leave through, a flight to my land,
would I make my finger a pencil, write
my name and address, any words I could round
up—"The Pied Piper" or a speech by Othello—
on the slate in my head, then erase and begin
again? Where would the light come in
to show me a stranger I might not want to know?

\*

*Bring on the familiar*
               I'd tell my memories
bead after bead, I'd replay
a cold night among the plotted stories
when a star drew its death across the sky . . .
how driving to the airport on a bitter day
I saw the seagull touch down, poise
on the lamppost, relax its wings, stay . . .
how someone was afraid and told me and I purposely
misunderstood . . .
               in the hour of my fear I pay.
I brush the shadows, hug the lifesize stills
of all who ever touched me, now propped between
my prison and the theater where hope unreels
and I am fed—like grain for Toulouse geese.

\*

There are people so lonely they call
a wrong number to hear a live voice
tell them Hello, Sorry. Or they dial
and yell Fire to hear sirens, an ax
slam through the flimsy door of their cell.
In mine, Father, what would I have for a face
without someone to see it? My body would cradle,
rock me to sleep. And if I got free

I might always draw a white line
inside me and walk it, between *yes*
and *no*. Solitude might never release
me to sing again in God's ear, or man's.

Where the river cleaves
our city from theirs
I watch from the sidewalk at 10 A.M.
him dart in front of the ranch wagon
which rocks to a stop
as he bends, disappears
behind the front fender

muttering, scoops up a handful
of something, covers it
with the dome of his palm,
zigzags onto the pavement
where the wind yanks
off his hat and drops it in traffic.

I'm reading his back
*Santucci Bros. Contractor*
wondering is it safe
to walk close when he

unlids what almost killed him—
two black bars in a yellow down face,
the most lost, puzzled duckling
that ever wanted its mama.

I hand him his hat.

*after photographs by Lewis Hine*

### Cannery Workers, Buffalo, New York

The fascination of beans! All eyes are on them
as the women and children perch on baskets,
shelling beans into barrels, into galvanized tin.
On the filthy floor, children go barefoot,
their toes small as beans cut from pods.
Who is this visitor? Three children dare peek,
one woman's eyes raise while her head
tilts efficiently down. Each second puts beans
in the basket, beans on her table. And the man
stands at the center in his clean white jacket,
dark fedora, smoking his pipe, looking down.
*His* hands? Clasped behind him.
The building exposes its ribs, its high grudging windows.
Ropes and pulleys hold still.
Hung in mid-air, a clothespin-size object
on string. A bell-pull? to bring down
the curtain? a finger
chopped by the honed shelling knife, an object lesson?
Close the door. Let them finish our beans.

### Breaker Boys, Pittston, Pennsylvania

In standard peaked caps they belong
to an army that reaches the rafters.
Their teachers are marking them absent,
their mothers are counting the change.
On this slope something's exploded
but no one looks up from his chute.
The dust of a battlefield hangs in the air
and columns of six-year-old boys
vanish inside it, pass through the wall.
Bent like musicians, all
play one rumbling instrument.
To strike it their fingers must bleed,
their spines curve like bentwood
seasoned ten hours a day.
The teenage conductor holds the baton.
But at the backs of his players?
As they pick out the pieces of stone
and slate that won't burn
fire is stoked in their shoulders.

They take poison each day
like a tonic. They are turned from
their boss, from the camera.
They are no one we know.

## Beggar, New York City

Feet cropped, she has nothing to stand on
—or the pavement has turned into quicksand.
Black thread in a furrow over her brows
pulls them up, lifts her gaze
toward a thing we can't see,
or toward nothing. Her lips part
but what can she say
that her form hasn't already shouted?
Besides, we're not out to hear.
Meanwhile, there's help
from this billboard which props her against its
"Pocket Edition Safety Razor, Known . . .
the World Over," the maker has paid it to say so.
While commerce talks to her back
her eyes ask the sky.
An empty delivery wagon
and the head of a horse wearing blinders
emerge from each side of the billboard.
The horse has to wait for a driver.
The beggar's hand rests like a paperweight
on the blanket around her. If
you or I turned the corner
the woman would show us her lifeline.
And then where would we all be?

*List All Interments for Record*

*Katherine Simmons, née O'Reilly,*
from County Longford, Ireland,
strange grandmother I only see
in this photo: your hands
square clasping a white apron, hips ample,
and beside you your sixth child, my father
leaning against you pudgy, dimpled—
both wearing smiles made of paper.

*Gary Edward Simmons,* seven days brother
slipped through the hole in your heart,
I look for you everywhere.
In that box, why wouldn't you start
to cry any minute, to kick your feet?
Through frosted glass, light
shone onto your red hair, your round cheeks.
I wasn't scared. Except you seemed so all right.

*Some Important Things to Know:*

*Not more than two flags on a plot. One must be
an American flag. Faded flags will be removed immediately.*

*Edward Thomas Simmons* of Manchester, England,
Grandfather, foreman of quarry and home
you were always old. How could we be friends?
Those Sunday afternoons, time
stretched taut as violin strings while we sat tall
over tea and cookies. We were closest
once at Central Park when, together, transfixed,
we watched the rhino unloose his bowel.

*Some Important Things to Know:*

*Strict observance of the decorum which should
characterize such a place will be required.*

*Edward Thomas Simmons, Junior,* you had to wear
a hand-me-down name.
Prize uncle, you rescued me from the parlor,
shutting the French doors between us and them.

Royal in your armchair, you doused
the light and began constructing a tale
that would keep me awake, tossed
on seas of fear. I loved each horrible
moment. Dear fellow exile: I disbelonged
because I was little. How were you wrong?

*Alvin J. Simmons,* postman, you hardly spoke.
You'd leave the room.
Maybe words broke your back,
so you wouldn't carry them home.
Outside, people called you funny.
We wondered was it you.

*Madeline Viola Simmons,* godmother of my moral
education should parents flunk
the course, you were my glamour girl
aunt dressed up for your job at the bank.
Underground at the Federal Reserve you sat in a "pool."
You'd had proposals but Grandpa always said No.
For fifty years' service, you got a watch, some annual
reports you'd typed. At six I begged to wear your shoes.

*Some Important Things to Know:*

*A few well-chosen plants will look best
and last longest.*

*Henry Reginald Simmons,* co-author
of me, I am not finished yet
talking to you. Listen: this summer
your two daughters bet
in a race in Sligo, Ireland
run the anniversary of your death
and that horse, Kilgarvin, won.
Now say it. Aren't you proud
of your girls, Reggie? Aren't you glad?

*Catherine Edwina Simmons,* firstborn, last gone
they said you almost ran away to study opera.
They said that when you sang
the neighbors threw their windows open.
Sometimes you took the train into the city.

Sometimes my father drove you here
so you could leave red tulips on the family plot.
I never heard you sing a note.

*Some Important Things to Know:*

*This is to certify*
*This deed is not assignable without consent*
*This plot is endowed for permanent care*